Viola or Cello
with Piano Accompaniment

SIX VERY EASY PIECES
in the First Position
Op. 22

EDWARD ELGAR

BOSWORTH

Exclusive distributors: Music Sales Limited,
Newmarket Road, Bury St. Edmunds, Suffolk IP33 3YB

Six Very Easy Pieces
(Op. 22)

1.

Viola with Piano Accompaniment
adapted by Michael Pope

EDWARD ELGAR

NOTE: [Composed for Violin and Piano in 1892, for the Composer's niece, May Grafton]

Imprimé en Angleterre
Made in England

Tous droits d'execution réservés

2.

4

3.

4.

5.

F.

Allegro.